DIESEL SHUNTERS

HUGH LLEWELYN

AMBERLEY

First published 2014

Amberley Publishing
The Hill, Stroud
Gloucestershire, GL5 4EP

www.amberley-books.com

Copyright © Hugh Llewelyn 2014

The right of Hugh Llewelyn to be identified as the Author
of this work has been asserted in accordance with the
Copyrights, Designs and Patents Act 1988.

All rights reserved. No part of this book may be reprinted
or reproduced or utilised in any form or by any electronic,
mechanical or other means, now known or hereafter invented,
including photocopying and recording, or in any information
storage or retrieval system, without the permission in writing
from the Publishers.

British Library Cataloguing in Publication Data.
A catalogue record for this book is available from the British Library.

ISBN 978 1 4456 3946 8 (print)
ISBN 978 1 4456 3957 4 (ebook)

Typeset in 10pt on 12pt Sabon.
Typesetting and Origination by Amberley Publishing.
Printed in the UK.

Contents

Introduction

As a child in a South Wales mining village in the late 1950s and early 1960s, the shunters I was familiar with were still steam. In the local colliery at Seven Sisters in the Dulais Valley there was a small Peckett 0-4-0ST, and in the nearby Onllwyn Washery was a variety of Austerity 0-6-0STs, a Peckett 0-6-0ST and even, for a time, an ex-GWR 16XX Class 0-6-0PT. The coal from the Dulais Valley largely went to Swansea Docks, where East Dock shed housed many 57XX Class 0-6-0PTs being used for shunting or trip work.

But then change came rapidly. Almost before I realised it, the several collieries in the Dulais Valley closed and with them went their shunters. At Swansea East Dock the pannier tanks were replaced by BR Class 03 and 08 0-6-0 diesel shunters while at Onllwyn the saddle tanks were replaced by English Electric 0-6-0s. Little did I realise that once the change from steam to diesel had taken place, even the era of diesel shunters would last a relatively short time compared to the long reign of steam. With the gradual contraction of the South Wales coal field, the coal traffic which once had dominated the local railway scene also diminished. Of the coal traffic that remained, most was carried in the new HAA hoppers in 'merry-go-round' trains that did not need shunting.

Although that picture of the lessening need for shunters – of any type – applies to South Wales, the general trend of declining wagon-load traffic was true everywhere in the UK. Thus, hardly had I got used to the change-over from steam to diesel than I noticed that some of the early pre-nationalisation diesel shunters were appearing in the various scrapyards alongside the last steam engines. I particularly remember seeing a rare ex-Southern Railway Maunsell-designed 0-6-0 diesel shunter being scrapped at Cashmore's, Newport.

Shunters at Swansea East Dock
In the days when large numbers of shunters were still needed in British docks a line of BR/English Electric Standard 400 hp 0-6-0 diesel electric shunters (later Class 08) and BR/Gardner Standard 204 hp Light 0-60 diesel mechanical shunters (later Class 03), all in BR green livery, await their next turn of duty at Swansea (East Dock), April 1967.

Nonetheless, despite the steady reduction of the diesel shunter fleet over the following decades, and the extinction of most of the numerous classes that BR had ordered, there are still substantial numbers of Class 08 and 09 standard shunters working on the privatised network, while many examples of most of the BR classes are preserved. Unfortunately, while in the 1960s many large stations had shunters acting as pilots and many stations of all sizes had sidings adjacent to them which allowed easy photography of shunters, all that has now gone and surviving shunters are usually in locations difficult to access.

A similar story applies to the need for industrial shunters as the UK entered the post-industrial era. With the number of industries using shunters having been drastically reduced since the 1960s, coupled with the inaccessibility of industrial sites, photography of working shunters is also very difficult. Moreover, despite there being a far greater variety of industrial shunters built compared to those for British Railways, relatively few types have been preserved compared to the BR classes, of which most have preserved examples.

Thus, the photographs in this book include a few of shunters operating with BR or the privatised companies, but most are of those BR and industrial shunters in preservation. I have also taken liberties and included a few petrol-engined shunters and shunters built in Britain for service abroad.

The humble diesel shunter has not received the same amount of attention that its more glamorous mainline siblings have, but in my view diesel shunters are just as photogenic. And, at least for me, there is a great deal of interest in the variety of designs produced – and they are British-built! Apart from those shunters built in BR workshops such as Crewe, Derby, Doncaster, Darlington and Swindon, many shunters of both BR and industry were designs produced by private companies – English Electric, Drewry, North British, Hunslet, Barclay, Hudswell Clarke, Yorkshire Engine, Ruston & Hornsby and so on. Oh, the glories of a once huge British locomotive industry! I hope this book reflects the proud legacy of that locomotive industry.

Hugh Llewelyn, 2014

D4016
BR/English Electric (later Class 08) 400 hp 0-6-0 No. D3503 (later No. 08 388) in a very grimy BR green livery shunting a mixture of parcels vans at Newton Abbot MPD, August 1966. Once, diesel shunters could be easily seen from the platforms of many British stations.

Early Pre-Nationalisation Shunters

LMS 7050
Preserved LMS 0-4-0 diesel mechanical shunter No. 7050, a Drewry design built by
English Electric's Dick Kerr works at Preston in 1934 for the LMS. In the Second World
War it was taken over by the War Department (as No. 846, then No. 70224 and finally
No. 224). Drewry Works No. 2047; EE Works No. 847. It was built with an Allan 8RS18
engine of 160 hp but was later refitted with a Gardner 6L3 of 153 hp. Photographed at
the National Railway Museum, York, in September 2010. In 1947 Drewry developed a
0-6-0 version of this as a demonstrator which was trialled by the LNER and became the
prototype of the BR Class 04.

7050 Nameplate

Drewry Works Plate of LMS/Drewry 0-4-0 diesel mechanical shunter LMS No. 7050, built at English Electric's Dick Kerr Works, Preston; at the National Railway Museum, York, September 2010. Drewry was a marketing/sales business and design bureau which sub-contracted construction of its designs to established locomotive builders, usually those belonging to the English Electric group.

LMS 7069

LMS English Electric/Hawthorn Leslie 350 hp diesel electric 0-6-0 shunter (EE/HL No. 3841 of 1935), LMS No. 7069. The engine is an English Electric 6K. In 1940 it was requisitioned by the War Department as their No. 18 and shipped to France. On the Fall of France, it was taken over by the Germans. After D-Day 1944, it was recaptured by the Allies and then used by the French, working at a General Reserve Munitions Depot until 1957, when it was sold to the Chemin de fer Mamers à St Calais as their No. 7 until 1972, when it fell into disuse. In 1973 it was sold to a loco dealers, who renovated it but found no buyer until it was bought for preservation in the UK in 1988. The photo shows 7069 under restoration in Toddington shed, Gloucestershire Warwickshire Railway (GWR), May 2013. Three sister locos had stayed in the UK in 1940 and eventually became BR Nos 12000–2, being withdrawn 1956–62.

15202
SR/English Electric R. E. L. Maunsell-designed diesel electric 350 hp 0-6-0 shunter No. 15202 (ex-SR No. 2) in BR green livery awaiting scrapping at Cashmore's Scrapyard, Newport, June 1967. This was one of three SR diesel shunters, none of which were preserved, from which the BR (SR) Bulleid Class 12 shunters evolved. The engine was an English Electric 6K. During the Second World War, these three shunters served with the War Department and were used on the Martin Mill Military Railway, hauling heavy guns (and ammunition) to fire across the English Channel. Diesel locomotives did not give away the guns' positions to German gunners in France.

British Railways Shunters

North British (Unclassified) Shunters

Preserved North British 0-4-0 diesel hydraulic shunter No. D2767 in BR green livery – but without an emblem – on a winter's day at Bury Shed, East Lancashire Railway, December 1989. The engine is a 225 hp NBL-MAN W6V 17.5/22A. This class was never included in the TOPS classification scheme even though three survived to the early 1970s. Of the numerous small 0-4-0 designs used by BR, this class was built in the largest numbers – seventy-three in 1957–61 – but the small yards for which they were intended disappeared rapidly and all were withdrawn in 1967–71.

Preserved North British 225 hp 0-4-0 diesel hydraulic shunter No. 2767 (ex-No. D2767) in BR Rail Blue livery on a cold winter's day at Bury Shed, East Lancashire Railway, December 1999.

Preserved North British 225 hp 0-4-0 diesel hydraulic shunter No. D2774 in BR green livery at Bury Shed, East Lancashire Railway, December 1999.

Hudswell Clarke (Unclassified) Shunters

Preserved Hudswell Clarke diesel mechanical 0-6-0 No. D2511 in BR green livery at Haworth on the Keighley & Valley Railway, May 1998. The engine is a 204 hp Gardner 8L3. They were built in two distinct groups, ten in 1955–56 specifically for dock-work and ten in 1961 for more general shunting. The former was a development of two 150 hp Mirlees Ricardo-engined Hudswell Clarke 0-6-0s for the LMS (Nos 7055 and 7066) of 1934 and had the traditional Hudswell steam locomotive outline and jackshaft drive from the rear – very unusual among builders who used jackshaft drive, which was normally from the front. The latter group used the same engine and mechanical parts but in a completely new, modern style with an off-centre cab and with the chassis turned around so that the jackshaft drive (somewhat dated for 1961) was at the front. Why this second batch was built at all is a mystery because the standard 204 hp 0-6-0 shunters of Class 03 and 04 were plentiful and were designed for the same duties. All twenty Hudswell Clarkes were withdrawn in 1967 as 'non-standard' although two saw further service with the NCB. The first time I saw one of this class, it was of the second batch and I could not understand why it looked completely unlike the photograph of the class in my Ian Allan Combined Volume – which was of the first group. Only years later did I learn of the 'split personality' of this supposedly single class design.

Class 01

Preserved Barclay Class 01 153 hp 0-4-0 diesel mechanical shunter No. 11506 (later D2956) in BR black livery and with 1949 emblem on a very cold day at Bury Shed, East Lancashire Railway, January 2000. The engine is a Gardner 6L3. Five were built in 1956–58 for dock lines and were withdrawn in 1966–81.

Class 02

Yorkshire Engine 170 hp diesel hydraulic 0-4-0 Class 02 No. D2860 (YE No. 2843 of 1961) in BR green livery at the National Railway Museum, York, August 1999. The engine is a Rolls-Royce C6. Thirty were built 1960–61 and were withdrawn 1969–75.

BR Standard Light Shunters, 204 hp 0-6-0 diesel mechanical shunters (later Class 03) Nos D2117 (later 03 117) and D2125 (later 03 125) in BR green livery and with flower pot exhausts at Swansea (East Dock), April 1967.

Preserved BR Class 03, 0-6-0 DM, No. D2117 in Haverthwaite yard in the livery of the Lakeside & Haverthwaite Railway as their No. 8, September 1973.

BR Class 03 204 hp diesel mechanical 0-6-0 No. 03 008 (ex-No. D2008; ex-No. 11195) with 'Saxa' chimney and in BR Rail Blue livery shunting at Cambridge, October 1995. The engine is a Garner 8L3. The design is a BR version of the Drewry Class 04. 230 were built 1957–62 at the BR Swindon and Doncaster works and BR withdrew them in 1967–93 although many were sold into private industry.

Preserved BR Class 03 204 hp 0-6-0 diesel mechanical shunter No. D2133 (later No. 03 133) with wide chimney in a blue livery and Courtaulds Films branding at Minehead, West Somerset Railway, July 1996.

Preserved BR Class 03 204 hp 0-6-0 No. D.2138 (later No. 03 138) with wide chimney and in BR green livery at the Midland Railway Centre, Butterley, Ripley, May 1998. Note full stop after 'D' and before number.

Preserved BR Class 03 204 hp 0-6-0 No. 11226 (later No. D2073; then No. 03 073) with wide chimney and in BR black livery at the Crewe Heritage Centre, October 1999.

Preserved BR Class 03 204 hp diesel mechanical 0-6-0 No. D2062 (ex-11215; later No. 03 073; then No. 03 062) with wide chimney and in BR green livery on a very cold day at Bury Shed, East Lancashire Railway, December 1999.

Preserved BR Class 03 204 hp 0-6-0 diesel mechanical shunter No. D 2138 (later No. 03 138) with wide chimney in BR green at the Midland Railway Centre, Butterley, June 1998.

Preserved BR Class 03 204 hp 0-6-0 shunter No. 03 066 (ex-D2066) in BR blue livery at Barrow Hill, April 2009.

Preserved BR Class 03 204 hp 0-6-0 diesel mechanical shunter No. D2133 (later 03 133) with wide chimney in BR green at Minehead, West Somerset Railway, October 2009.

Preserved BR Class 03 204 hp 0-6-0 No. 03 119 (ex-D2119) with cut-down cab for working on the Burry Port & Gwendraeth Valley line, South Wales, and in BR blue livery. It has a wide chimney. At Williton, West Somerset Railway, September 2010.

Class 04

Drewry Class 04 204 hp 0-6-0 shunter No. D2309 (ex-No. 11289) in BR green livery with a 'Saxa' chimney at York Shed, July 1967.

Preserved Drewry Class 04 204 hp 0-6-0 diesel mechanical shunter No. 11230 (later D2260; then No. 04 260) in early BR black livery at Long Marston, June 2009. It has a 'Saxa' type chimney. Its engine is a Gardner 8L3. As the Drewry Car Co. was a sales/marketing company and design bureau and not a builder, the production run of 141 locos were built by Robert Stephenson & Hawthorns and the Vulcan Foundry in 1952–61, although the prototype had been built as a demonstrator in 1947 (developed from the LMS 0-4-0 prototype No. 7050 of 1934) and had been used by the LNER. Together with the Class 03, essentially a BR-built version of the 04, these classes were the standard light 0-6-0 shunter for BR and were highly successful. The 04s were withdrawn earlier than the 03s, however, between 1967 and 1979, although many then served in private industry, especially the coal and steel industry.

Preserved Drewry Class 04 204 hp 0-6-0 shunter No. D2302 (it was never renumbered in the 04 series) in BR green livery with a 'Saxa' chimney at Barrow Hill, April 2009.

Preserved Drewry Class 04 204 hp 0-6-0 No. D2302 (never renumbered in the 04 series) in BR green and with 'Saxa' chimney at Barrow Hill, August 2008.

Preserved Drewry Class 04 204 hp 0-6-0 diesel mechanical shunter No. D2271 with narrow 'Saxa' chimney in BR Rail Blue at Minehead, WSR, October 2009. Built in 1958; after withdrawal in 1968, D2271 went into industrial use, being bought by C. F. Booth for depot use. It was later refurbished by Thomas Hill. It was finally withdrawn and preserved in 1979.

Class 05

Preserved Hunslet Class 05 204 hp diesel mechanical 0-6-0 No. D2587 (Hunslet No. 5636 of 1959; rebuilt Hunslet No. 7180 in 1969) in BR green livery at Barrow Hill, April 2012. The engine is a Gardner 8L3. This loco is of the second series, with a taller cab and extra side window above the others. Sixty-nine were built 1955–61 and were withdrawn 1966–68, except for one which survived on the Isle of Wight until 1981. Many were subsequently sold into private industry, usually coal and steel.

Class 07

Preserved Ruston & Hornsby Class 07 275 hp 0-6-0 No. D2944 (later 07 010) in BR green livery departing Bitton on an Oldland service on the Avon Valley Railway, May 2009. The 07s were built specially for use in Southampton Docks and were not painted in the standard Brunswick Green BR used for locomotives but in SR Coaching Stock Green because the Class was expected to haul boat trains into the docks and would thus match the coaches. Moreover, the standard BR locomotive 'lion-and-wheel' emblem was not used; the coaching stock emblem was, although the standard emblem would not have fitted on the cab side in any case.

BR/English Electric Standard 400 hp diesel electric 0-6-0 shunter No. D3503 (later No. 08 388) in BR green livery at Bristol (Bath Road) MPD, *c.* summer 1963. These became Class 08 under TOPS.

BR/English Electric Standard 400 hp 0-6-0 diesel electric shunter (later Class 08) No. D3758 later No. 08 591) in BR green livery and carrying snow/ballast ploughs at Swansea (East Dock), April 1967. It was rare for Class 08s to have ballast ploughs.

BR/English Electric 400hp Class 08 0-6-0 No. 13029 (later D3029; then No. 08 021) in 1949 BR black livery, emblem and number, preserved, at Tyseley, September 2010. The engine is an English Electric 6KT. Developed from the LMS/EE 350 hp shunter (Class 11), 996 Class 08s were built from 1952 to 1962 in the BR workshops at Crewe, Derby, Darlington, Doncaster and Harwich. Withdrawals began in 1967 but there are many still shunting on the privatised network and on industrial sites, aside from those being used by preserved railways.

BR/English Electric Class 08 400 hp 0-6-0 No. 08 542 (ex-No. D3706) in BR Rail Blue livery, acting as station pilot at Liverpool Street, August 1985.

BR/English Electric Class 08 400 hp 0-6-0 No. 08 850 (ex-No. D4018), with unusually small numerals, in BR Rail Blue livery at Minehead, West Somerset Railway, July 1994.

BR/English Electric Class 08 400 hp 0-6-0 No. 08 590 (ex-No. D3757), un-numbered and for some reason in BR black livery (which it never carried) at the Midland Railway Centre, Butterley, Ripley, May 1998.

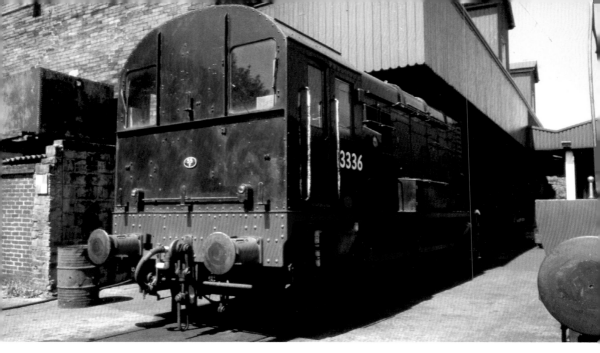

BR/English Electric 400 hp Class 08 0-6-0 No. 13336 (later No. D3336; subsequently No. 08 266) in 1949 BR black livery, preserved, at Haworth Shed on the Keighley & Worth Valley Railway, June 1998.

BR/English Electric Class 08 400 hp 0-6-0 No. 08 643 (ex-No. D3810) in BR Railfreight Grey with a brake van approaching Bristol Temple Meads, May 1992.

Preserved BR/English Electric Class 08 400 hp 0-6-0 No. D4157 (later No. 08 927) in BR green livery, making brake van trips at Toddington, Gloucestershire-Warwickshire Railway, March 2010.

BR/English Electric Class 08 400 hp 0-6-0 No. 08 517 (ex-No. D3679) in very badly faded BR blue awaiting scrapping at Motorail Logistics, Long Marston, September 2010.

BR/EE Class 08 400 hp 0-6-0 No. 08 492 (ex-No. D3607) of Harry Needle Railway Co. in BR Rail Blue livery, supposedly in store at Barrow Hill, August 2008.

BR/English Electric Class 08 0-6-0 No. 08 869 (ex-No. D4037) of Harry Needle Railroad Company in BR blue livery, supposedly in store but probably awaiting scrapping at Motorail Logistics, Long Marston, September 2010.

BR/English Electric Class 08 400 hp 0-6-0 No. 08 867 (ex-No. D4037) in BR blue awaiting scrapping at Motorail Logistics, Long Marston, September 2010. Note very small numbers.

BR/English Electric Class 08 400 hp 0-6-0 No. 08 813 (ex-No. D3981), minus centre axle, of HNRC in faded BR departmental grey, allegedly in store but more probably awaiting scrapping at Long Marston, September 2010.

BR/English Electric Class 08 400 hp 0-6-0 No. 08 827 (ex-No. D3995) of HNRC in badly faded BR blue, supposedly in store but in reality awaiting scrapping at Long Marston, September 2010.

BR/English Electric Class 08 400 hp 0-6-0 No. 08 728 (ex-No. D3896) in Deanside Transit-branded BR blue livery at Long Marston, June 2009.

Although showing no number, I think this is BR/English Electric Class 08 400 hp 0-6-0 No. 08 447 (ex-No. D3562) *Russell* of Russell Engineering, Hillington, Glasgow, in yellow livery (and half a coupling rod) at Long Marston, June 2009.

BR/English Electric Class 08 400 hp 0-6-0 No. 08 736 (ex-No. D3904) in Deanside Transit-branded BR blue livery at Long Marston, June 2009.

BR/English Electric Class 08 400 hp 0-6-0 shunter No. 08 899 (ex-No. D4129) of East Midlands Trains in Maintrain blue livery at Derby, July 2008.

BR/English Electric Class 08 400 hp 0-6-0 No. 08 869 (ex-No. D4037) in BR blue livery at Long Marston, June 2009.

Above: BR/English Electric Class 08 400 hp 0-6-0 shunter No. 08 908 (ex-No. D4138) of East Midlands Trains but still, more or less, in Midland Main Line livery, though with different coloured panels, possibly from other locos, at Derby, July 2008.

Opposite above: BR/English Electric Class 08 400 hp 0-6-0 No. 08 695 (ex- No. D3862) of HNRC in EWS livery at Barrow Hill, August 2008.

Opposite below: Preserved BR/English Electric Class 08 400 hp 0-6-0 No. 08 683 (ex-No. D3850), still in EWS livery at Toddington, GWR, June 2010.

Preserved BR/English Electric Class 08 400 hp 0-6-0 shunter No. 604 (ex-No. 08 064; then No. D3771) *Phantom* in mock GWR green livery with GWR style number and nameplates at Didcot, May 2010.

BR/English Electric Class 08 400 hp 0-6-0 No. 08 757 (ex-No. D3925) of DBS, amazingly still in BR Parcels livery at Didcot Yard, April 2011.

BR/English Electric Class 08 400 hp 0-6-0 shunter No. 08 697 (ex-No. D3864) of East Midlands Trains, still in BR blue livery at Derby, July 2008.

BR/English Electric Class 08 400 hp 0-6-0 No. 08 492 (ex-No. D3607) of HNRC in BR blue livery in store at Barrow Hill, April 2009.

Class 09

BR/English Electric Class 09/0 400 hp diesel electric 0-6-0 No. 09 001 (ex-No. D3665) in Rail Blue livery, acting as station pilot at Waterloo, November 1975. The engine is an English Electric 6KT. The Class 09s were simply a re-geared Class 08 to allow a higher speed and all were allocated to the Southern Region; twenty-six were built in 1959–1962 at Darlington and Horwich. In 1992, seven Class 08s were converted to Class 09/1 and another five to Class 09/2.

Preserved BR/English Electric Class 09 400 hp 0-6-0 No. 09 012 *Dick Hardy* (ex-No. D4100), recently withdrawn by DBS, in BR departmental grey and black livery at Barrow Hill, April 2012.

Class 10

BR/Blackstone (later Class 10) 350 hp 0-6-0 shunter No. D3634 (never renumbered in 10 series) in BR green at Stratford MPD, July 1967.

Preserved BR/Blackstone Class 10 diesel electrical 350 hp 0-6-0 shunter No. D3452 (never renumbered in 10 series) in BR black livery at Bodmin General, Bodmin & Wenford Railway, August 1995. The engine is a Blackstone ER6T. 146 were built 1953–62 at BR's Darlington and Doncaster workshops plus fifteen very similar locos with different traction motors (scrapped before TOPS classification) in 1955 by BR Darlington Works.

Preserved BR/Blackstone Class 10 350 hp 0-6-0 shunter No. D4067 *Margaret Ethel – Thomas Alfred Naylor* (never renumbered in 10 series) in BR in what appears to be a very badly faded BR green livery at Loughborough, Great Central Railway, October 1999.

Preserved BR/Blackstone Class 10 350 hp 0-6-0 shunter No. D4092 (never renumbered in 10 series) in BR green at Barrow Hill, August 2008.

BR/Blackstone (later Class 10) 350 hp 0-6-0 shunter No. D3970 (never renumbered in 10 series) in BR green livery at an open day in Ashford, October 1972.

LMS/English Electric 350 hp 0-6-0 diesel shunter (later Class 11) No. 12104 in BR green livery at Stratford MPD, July 1967.

LMS/English Electric 350 hp 0-6-0 diesel electric shunter (later Class 11) No. 12077 in BR green livery at the Midland Railway Centre, Butterley, Ripley, May 1998. The engine is an English Electric 6K. Between 1945 and 1952 120 were built by the LMS/BR's works at Derby and BR's works at Darlington. 106 went to the LMS (including six ordered by the War Department that went straight to the LMS) and BR while fourteen went to the WD and then were sold to the NS (Netherlandshe Spoorwegen) in 1946.

LMS/English Electric 350 hp 0-6-0 diesel shunter (later Class 11) No. 12131 in BR black livery at Weybourne, North Norfolk Railway, July 1999. 120 were built by the LMS and BR at Derby and Darlington.

Class 14

BR Class 14 650 hp diesel hydraulic 0-6-0 No. D9553 in BR two-tone green livery at Toddington, GWR, August 1995. The engine is a Paxman Ventura 6YJXL. Designed by the Western Region's CME, R. A. Smeddle, the Class 14s were based on the German V80 B-Bs. Swindon Works built fifty-six in 1964–65 for heavy shunting, transfer 'trip' freight, branch freight and local main-line freight but by the time the engines were built, these duties were disappearing rapidly with the result that all were withdrawn in 1967–69 – an incredibly short life with BR. However, most were sold into private industry – the coal, steel, quarry and oil industries. No. D9553 served with the British Steel Corporation and the number '54' is that of BSC, who operated the loco from 1968 until the early 1980s in the East Midlands ironstone quarries.

Preserved BR (Swindon) Class 14 650 hp 0-6-0 No. D9526 in BR two-tone green at Williton shed, WSR, September 2010. After withdrawal by BR, D9526 was bought by Associated Portland Cement Manufacturing and used at their Westbury Works.

Preserved BR (Swindon) Class 14 650 hp 0-6-0 No. D9520 in BR two-tone green livery with a shuttle on the branch at Barrow Hill, August 2008. After withdrawal, it was bought by the British Steel Corporation (as No. 45) and served at Glendon East, then Corby.

Class 20

Above: Now in industrial service as a shunter at the Hope Cement Works, English Electric Class 20/0 1,000 hp Bo-Bo No. 20 168 (ex-D8168) of Lafarge Cement, in their very attractive green and white livery, is ready to pull out of the Hope Works for Earles' Sidings, September 2008. The loco was later named *Sir George Earle*, the founder of the works.

Opposite bottom: English Electric Class 20/0 diesel electric 1,000 hp Bo-Bo No. 2017 (ex-20 088; D8088), after withdrawal by RFS Engineering, Doncaster, in RFS livery awaiting scrapping at Long Marston, September 2010. The engine is an English Electric 8SVT. The standard BR Type 1, between 1957 and 1968 228 were built. Although intended for main line and local freight services, after withdrawal from BR several went to serve in private industry for heavy shunting. So reliable is the design that many are still serving on the privatised network.

Industrial Shunters

Bagnall Shunters

Preserved Bagnall 0-6-0 No. 3150 of 1959, fitted with a 204 hp Gardner engine and mechanical transmission. It was used by the NCB at Woolstanton Colliery, Stoke-on-Trent, as *Wolstanton No. 3*. It was typical of the Bagnall diesel shunters used by the NCB in Staffordshire, and is seen at the Foxfield Light Railway, October 1999.

Brush-Bagnell Shunters

Brush-Bagnall 480 hp 0-6-0 diesel-electric shunter (second batch) No. 3002 of 1951, British Steel Corporation (originally Steel Company of Wales) No. 703, on shed at the Abbey Works, Port Talbot, September 1969. Inspired by the LMS/BR/EE 400 hp 0-6-0 diesel shunters, the Brush-Bagnall shunters for SCOW were built in two batches:

Nos 2971–4 of 1951-3, 2971 to Lever Brothers, Port Sunlight (later used by a contractor to dismantle railways in mid-Wales), 2972–74 to SCOW, Abbey Works, Port Talbot as Nos 713 (initially SCOW Trostre Tinplate Works, Llanelli No. 2), 711, 712, with Mirrlees 6-cyl TLT6 engine of 355 hp;

Nos 3000–3 of 1951, SCOW Abbey Works Nos 701, 702, 703, 704 (initially SCOW Trostre Tinplate Works, Llanelli, No. 1), with Mirrlees TLST6 of 480 hp.

Many similar locomotives with Mirrlees or National engines were subsequently built for industrial uses – but none for BR.

Brush-Bagnall 300 hp 0-4-0 diesel-electric shunter (1st batch) No. 3066 of 1954, British Steel Corporation (originally Steel Company of Wales) No. 501, on shed at the Abbey Works, Port Talbot, September 1969. Designed for lighter duties at SCOW's steel/tinplate works, these locos were built in two batches:

3066–72 of 1954–55, SCOW Abbey Works Nos 501–07, with 300 hp National M4AAU6 6-cyl engine;

3096–3103/3120 of 1956, SCOW Trostre Tinplate Works, Llanelli No. 1, SCOW Velindre Tinplate Works No. LD1, SCOW Abbey Works Nos 508–14 with 300 hp National M4AAU6 engine.

Some of both batches were later rebuilt with 335 hp Rolls-Royce engines.

This design became the standard 'heavy' 0-4-0 diesel shunter of Brush, who continued building them after the dissolution of Brush-Bagnall, sometimes in association with Beyer Peacock.

Brush-Bagnall 515 hp Bo-Bo diesel-electric shunter (first batch) No. 3065 of 1955, British Steel Corporation (originally Steel Company of Wales) No. 903, shunting at the Abbey Works, Port Talbot, September 1969. Designed for heavy duties at SCOW's steel works to supplement five ALCO Bo-Bos bought in 1950, more purchases of which were prevented by post-war import controls. Three batches were built to the larger US loading gauge of the railway system of the Abbey Works:

3063–5 of 1955, SCOW Abbey Works Nos 901–03, with a 515 hp Mirrlees J6 6-cyl engine;

3111–3 of 1956–7, SCOW Abbey Works Nos 951–53, with a 750 hp Mirrlees JS6 6-cyl engine. In 1992/3 three (907–9) were rebuilt by Hunslet-Barclay, Kilmarnock, with a Perkins engine.

3137–3143 of 1957, SCOW Abbey Works Nos 904–10, which reverted to the unsupercharged 515 hp Mirrlees J6 engine but had the deeper, heavier frames of the second batch.

Brush-Bagnall 335 hp 0-4-0 diesel-electric shunter (2nd batch, re-engined) No. 3101 of 1956, British Steel Corporation (originally Steel Company of Wales) No. 511, on shed at the Abbey Works, Port Talbot, September 1969. Designed for lighter duties at SCOW's steel/tinplate works, these locos were built in two batches:

3066–72 of 1954–55, SCOW Abbey Works Nos 501–07, with 300 hp National M4AAU6 6-cyl engine;

3096–3103/3120 of 1956, SCOW Trostre Tinplate Works, Llanelli No. 1, SCOW Velindre Tinplate Works No. LD1, SCOW Abbey Works Nos 508–14 with 300 hp National M4AAU6 engine.

Some of both batches were later rebuilt with 335 hp Rolls Royce engines.

This design became the standard 'heavy' 0-4-0 diesel shunter of Brush, who continued building then after the dissolution of Brush-Bagnall, sometimes in association with Beyer Peacock.

Brush-Bagnall 750 hp Bo-Bo diesel-electric shunter (second batch) No. 3112 of 1957, British Steel Corporation (originally Steel Company of Wales) No. 952, at the Abbey Works, Port Talbot, September 1969. Designed for heavy duties at SCOW's steel works to supplement five ALCO Bo-Bos bought in 1950, more of which were prevented by post-war import controls. Three batches were built to the larger US loading gauge of the railway system of the Abbey Works:

3063–5 of 1955, SCOW Abbey Works Nos 901–03, with a 515 hp Mirrlees J6 6-cyl engine;

3111–3 of 1956–7, SCOW Abbey Works Nos 951–53, with a 750 hp Mirrlees JS6 6-cyl engine. In 1992/3 three (907–9) were rebuilt by Hunslet-Barclay, Kilmarnock, with a Perkins engine.

3137–3143 of 1957, SCOW Abbey Works Nos 904–10, which reverted to the unsupercharged 515 hp Mirrlees J6 engine but had the deeper, heavier frames of the second batch.

Brush-Bagnall 515 hp Bo-Bo diesel-electric shunter (third batch) No. 3140 of 1958, British Steel Corporation (originally Steel Company of Wales) No. 907, at the Abbey Works, Port Talbot, September 1969. Designed for heavy duties at SCOW's steel works to supplement five ALCO Bo-Bos bought in 1950, more purchases of which were prevented by post-war import controls. Three batches were built to the larger US loading gauge of the railway system of the Abbey Works.

Barclay Shunters

Western Australian Government Railway 3-foot 6-inch gauge 0-4-0 diesel mechanical shunter No. 4, built by Andrew Barclay (works No. 317) in 1927 with a 45 hp four-cylinder Dorman Long petrol engine, which was replaced by a 68 hp Ford diesel in 1961. First used at Esperence, it was transferred in 1928 to Perth, where it worked at the WAGR workshops at Midland Junction until withdrawal in 1976, when it was transferred to the Bassendean Railway Museum, restored to working order and used on the site. Note works plate in centre of cab front! At the West Australian Railway Museum, Bassendean, Perth, February 2010.

Preserved Barclay 35t 0-4-0 diesel hydraulic No. 579 of 1972 (behind is No. 578) with 302 hp Paxman 6RPHL Mk7 engine. Built for MoD and worked at Royal Ordnance Depot, Puritan. At West Somerset Railway, Dunster, March 2010.

Barclay 0-4-0 shunter No. 70047 *Mulberry*. Built by Andrew Barclay, Kilmarnock (No. 362 of 1942), as a standard War Department shunter. 150 hp Gardner engine. Used in France 1944–46, and the Middle East 1952–55. At Long Marston, June 2009.

Preserved Barclay 0-4-0 diesel mechanical shunter No. 446 of 1959, *Kingswood*, with a 150 hp Gardner 6L3 six-cylinder engine; at Avon Valley Railway, Bitton, December 2012. The loco worked at the CEGB Rogerstone power station.

Drewry Shunters

This appears to be a Drewry 0-6-0 diesel mechanical shunter similar to BR Class 04, in which case it would have had a 204 hp Gardner engine. The photograph was taken in a South Wales colliery or industrial site in 1969. The only identification on the loco is a plate on the side of the nose which, under a looking glass, seems to be a standard 'Registered by the British Transport Commission' which clearly shows the date 1952, but the number is very indistinct; it could be 1872 but only the '8' is clear. I don't think this is an ex-BR Class 04 loco because of the BTC plate. From information received, it is possibly Drewry No. 2252 of 1948, built at Vulcan Foundary works No. D78 and working at Alcan Industries, Rogerstone.

Above: Preserved Baguley-Drewry 153 hp Gardner L3 engined 0-4-0 Drewry No. 2157 of 1941. Built by English Electric (Works No. 1188) and used by the War Department as No. WD 820. It took part in the Normandy Landings in 1944 and worked in France. Photographed at the Foxfield Light Railway, October 1999.

Opposite top: Baguley-Drewry 0-4-0 diesel hydraulic No. 3732 (though some sources say it is No. 3730) of 1977 *Tan Go* at Long Marston, September 2010.

Opposite bottom: Ex-BR Drewry Class 04 204 hp 0-6-0 shunter No. D2244 (ex-No. 11214) in blue livery with a 'Saxa' chimney, now in NCB use at Coedcae Colliery, March 1971.

Preserved Drewry/Robert Stephenson & Hawthorns 153 hp Gardner 6L3 engined 0-4-0 Drewry No. 2503 and RSH No. 7816 *Thalia* of 1954. It has two works numbers because, although Drewry designed shunters, they built none, contracting out construction to established locomotive companies, usually those belonging to the English Electric group. Pictured at Chatham Historic Dockyard, August 1999.

Preserved Drewry/Robert Stephenson & Hawthorns 153 hp Gardner 6L3 engined 0-4-0 Drewry No. 2589, and RSH No. 7922 of 1956. Built for the Dover Gas Works as *Harry*, it later went to Purfleet Deep Wharf and eventually to HNRC at Barrow Hill. It has two works numbers because, although Drewry designed shunters, they built none, contracting out construction to established locomotive companies, mainly those of the English Electric group. August 2008.

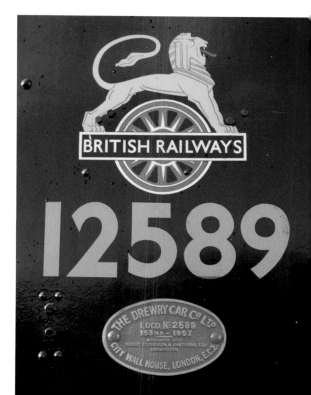

This seems to be a BR Drewry 0-4-0 shunter, No. 12589, but in fact BR had no Drewry 0-4-0s, only the Class 04, and they were 0-6-0s, and no BR diesel was numbered 12589! It is in fact the number of preserved Drewry/Robert Stephenson & Hawthorns' 0-4-0 Drewry No. 2589 and RSH No. 7922 of 1956, , at Barrow Hill, February 2014. The number is in 'gilt' (more a pale cream/straw colour) and in the LNER Gill Sans style as introduced by Thompson in 1945, but modified by Peppercorn in 1946 into a less condensed style. Below the BR number is the Drewry works plate and above is the 1949 BR emblem, commonly nicknamed the 'lion-on-a-unicycle'!

Works plate of preserved Drewry 0-4-0 Drewry No. 2589 (and Robert Stephenson & Hawthorns No. 7922) of 1956, *Harry*, at Barrow Hill, February 2014.

Preserved Drewry 0-4-0 diesel mechanical shunter (Drewry Works No. 2583), built by English Electric's Vulcan Foundary (Works No. D297) in 1956, in a garden at Wymondham, June 2008. Note tramway shrouds.

Although preserved as BR Class 03 204 hp 0-6-0 diesel mechanical shunter No. 11230 (later No. D2069, then No. 03 069) with 'Saxa' chimney in BR 1949 black livery, this is actually Drewry Works No. 2574, built in 1956 by Robert Stephenson & Hawthorns, Works No. 7860, for the NCB. At Winchcombe, Gloucestershire–Warwickshire Railway, May 2013.

English Electric Shunters

English Electric 0-6-0 diesel hydraulic 385 hp shunter, EE works No. D909 of 1964, built at the Vulcan Foundry, pictured at Garw International Colliery, Blaengarw, Afon Garw Valley, September 1969. It, together with sister No. 8429 of 1963 (built at the former Robert Stephenson & Hawthorns' Darlington works), also shunted at nearby Ffaldy Colliery. I drove No. D909 between the two collieries!

Preserved English Electric (Vulcan Foundary) 0-6-0 diesel electric shunter No. D226, *Vulcan*, with 500 hp EE 6RKT engine at Haworth Shed on the Keighley & Worth Valley Railway, April 1993. Nos D226 and sister D227 (which had hydraulic transmission for comparison purposes) were development locos built in 1956 and loaned to BR in 1959.

English Electric 0-6-0 diesel hydraulic shunter No. D1249 of 1968, rebuilt in 1971. It has a 550 hp Dorman V8 engine. Built for British Steel to work at their Llanwern steel works as *No. 104 Llanwern*. At Blaenavon Furnace Sidings, Pontypool & Blaenavon Railway, September 2011.

English Electric prototype 550 hp 0-6-0 diesel hydraulic heavy shunter No. D1226 of 1968, rebuilt in 1971 with a Dorman V8 engine. Used at British Steel's Llanwern steel works, where it was numbered No. 160. At Blaenavon Furnace Sidings, September 2011. The first of her class.

English Electric 0-6-0 diesel hydraulic No. D1233 of 1968 No. 2, *Kemira*, built at the Vulcan Foundary, stored at Long Marston September 2010.

GEC/English Electric 0-6-0 diesel hydraulic *Hippo*, No. 5352 of 1971, built at the Vulcan Foundary, seen at Long Marston September 2010. Owned by HNRC, though it had been on hire to RMS Locotec, Dewsbury.

English Electric 0-6-0 diesel hydraulic shunter, built at the Vulcan Foundary in 1967, works No. D1199, and rebuilt by Yorkshire Engine in 1996 for Thames Steel Ltd's Sheerness Steelworks, Isle of Sheppy, their No. L127 *Bill*. Now withdrawn, at Barrow Hill, April 2012.

English Electric 0-6-0 diesel hydraulic shunter, built at the Vulcan Foundary in 1967, works No. D1200, and rebuilt by Yorkshire Engine in 1996 for Thames Steel Ltd's Sheerness Steelworks, Isle of Sheppey, their No. L149, *Ben*. Now withdrawn at Barrow Hill, April 2012.

English Electric 0-6-0 diesel hydraulic RRM22, English Electric's works No. D1231 of 1967, built at the Vulcan Foundary. At Long Marston September 2010.

Fowler Shunters

Above: Fowler 200 hp 0-4-0 diesel mechanical shunter No. 22933, at Hay's Scrapyard, Bridgend, *c.* 1965. It was used by Hayes to haul withdrawn locos around the yard to be scrapped. This loco was of standard Fowler design and the number indicates it was probably built in the early 1940s. It probably had a Fowler 150 hp four-cylinder engine. The Engineering Department of the LMS had one of these machines (No. ED7) dating from 1940 and BR (LMR) ordered five more identical machines (Nos ED2–6), built in 1949. The SR had another (No. DS600), built in 1943, which was works shunter at Eastleigh. This too survived well into BR days.

Below: Fowler 0-4-0 diesel mechanical shunter No. 1455 of 1955, working on the standard gauge network of the Blue Circle Cement Works at Penarth, early 1968. This loco was mainly used to shunt coal wagons to fire the kilns. This design was the standard Fowler 4-foot 8.5-inch gauge diesel shunter (although engines varied, e.g. 88 hp Ruston and 70 hp MAN) and originated in the 1930s. Both the LMS and the GWR had one each, the former surviving to BR days.

2-foot 6-inch gauge Fowler 100 hp 0-4-0 diesel shunter No. 4160004 of 1951, *Blue Circle No. 4*, working on the then extensive narrow gauge network of the Blue Circle Cement Works at Penarth between limestone quarries and the works and kilns. The loco was dumped out of use in early 1968. It and its two sisters (No. 4160005 *Blue Circle No. 5* and No. 4160006 *Blue Circle No. 3*) were being replaced by dumper trucks at this time. This loco was mainly used to shunt coal wagons to fire the kilns.

Fowler 0-4-0 diesel mechanical shunter No. 4100001 of 1945, *Doctor Harry*, at Sheringham, North Norfolk Railway, April 1976.

Hibberd (Planet) Shunters

Hibbard Planet 4wd petrol mechanical shunter No. 2895 of 1944, to a design dating back to the First World War. It is of very low power. At the Electric Railway Museum, Coventry, September 2011.

Hudswell Clarke Shunters

What appears to be a standard Hudswell Clarke 0-6-0 diesel mechanical shunter is in fact a unique and highly unusual prototype demonstrator, No. D810 of 1958, *Enterprise*. Although the bodywork is standard, the engine is anything but; it was built as a normally aspirated Paxman 6RPH but was then fitted with a Brown Boveri turbocharger and extensively modified to work on Paxman's Hi-Dyne principle, which was intended to produce maximum power output and torque at low speed – which was more achievable with expensive hydraulic or electric transmission rather than cheaper mechanical transmissions. The transmission fitted to No. D810 was an experimental Fluidrive mechanical transmission. Unfortunately, the modifcations resulted in a reduction in power of the standard normally aspirated engine from 275 hp to 210 hp, which negated many of the advantages of the Hi-Dyne principle. The loco worked at various collieries and steel works. The only order which followed was for twenty-four 2-foot 6-inch gauge 2-8-2 mixed traffic locomotives (even though the Hi-Dyne principle was specifically designed for shunters) for the Sierra Leone Government Railways, built in 1957–61. The locomotives proved highly unreliable despite many modifications and the Hi-Dyne principle was shown to be a failure. No. D810 is pictured in 'as withdrawn' condition, at the Ashford Steam Centre, Otober 1972, the last time its existence is recorded.

Hudswell Clarke 0-6-0 diesel mechanical shunter No. D615 of 1938 with a McLaren-Benz 150 hp engine. Built for Shell-BP and named *Shell Mex – BP No. 14*. Preserved at Blaenavon Furnace Sidings on the Pontypool & Blaenavon Railway, September 2011.

Hudswell Clarke 0-6-0 diesel mechanical shunter, Works No. D1171, built in 1959 for the Port of Bristol Authority to work the Bristol Harbour branch, taking coal to the Western Power coal depot at Wapping Wharf. Very similar to the BR D2500 Class (none survived long enough to get a TOPS classification) 0-6-0 built by Hudswell Clarke with a 204 hp Gardner 6L3 engine. At Long Marston, June 2009.

Preserved Hudswell Clarke 0-6-0 diesel mechanical shunter, Works No. D1076, built in 1958 at Bury Shed, East Lancashire Railway, December 1990. It was Manchester Ship Canal No. 4002 *Arundel Castle*.

Preserved Hudswell Clarke 0-4-0 diesel hydraulic shunter No. D1387 of 1967 with 300 hp Cummins engine at Blaenavon Furnace Sidings shed, September 2011. It was used by the NCB at Bolsover Colliery until withdrawal in the early 1990s.

Hunslet Shunters

What appears to be a preserved Hunslet Class 05, 0-6-0 No. DL26, ostensibly as a BR departmental loco (in early BR black). In reality this particular loco, Works No. 5238, was one of four built by Hunslet in 1962 with a more powerful 264 hp National engine rather than the 05's 204 hp Gardner. Two of the four had hydraulic transmission (both for NCB) and two mechanical (one for Caltex, Istanbul, the other – DL26 – for the NCB). No. DL26 was used at Pleasby (twice), Bolsover and Blackwell collieries. At Didcot, November 2008.

Hunslet 'Snibstone' Class 0-6-0 diesel hydraulic No. 7276 of 1972, fitted with a 388 hp Cummins 400T engine. It was used by the NCB at Fryston Collery in Yorkshire before being bought by the Harry Needle Railroad Company and is shown in store at Motorail Logistics, Long Marston, September 2010.

Opposite top: Hunslet 0-4-0 diesel hydraulic No. 7161 of 1970, Fleetwood Department No. 2, at Long Marston, September 2010.

Opposite bottom: Hunslet 'Snibstone' Class 0-6-0 diesel hydraulic shunter No. 7181 of 1972, No. 28, with 388 hp Cummins 400T engine, at Long Marston, September 2010. It worked for the NCB at Littleton Colliery, Staffs.

Hunslet 0-6-0 diesel hydraulic No. 6614 of 1965; it has a 311 hp engine. It worked at the NCB Northumberland & Durham Division as No. 503; now in store at Long Marston, September 2010.

Hunslet Works Plate of Hunslet 0-6-0 diesel hydraulic No. 6614 of 1965 at Long Marston, September 2010.

Railway Executive Plate of Hunslet 'Snibstone' Class 0-6-0 diesel hydraulic No. 6614 of 1965 at Long Marston, September 2010. I'm not quite sure what a plate dated 1953 was doing on a loco built in 1965! The plates were affixed to locos in private industry that worked on the British Railways network.

Hunslet 0-6-0 diesel hydraulic *Rachael*, Works No. 7003, of 1971. It shunted at the Longbridge Plant of MG-Rover until it closed in 2007. At Long Marston, September 2010.

Above: Hunslet 0-6-0 diesel hydraulic *Emma*, Works No. 8902, of 1978. At Long Marston, September 2010. *Emma* worked at the MG-Rover plant at Longbridge until closure in 2007.

Opposite top: Hunslet 'Snibstone' Class 0-6-0 diesel hydraulic No. 6973 of 1969, National Smokeless Fuels No. 7, then owned by Harry Needle Railroad Company, at Barrow Hill, April 2009. It has a 388 hp Cummins 400T engine.

Opposite bottom: Hunslet 800 hp 0-8-0 diesel hydraulic heavy shunter No.D7063 of 1971 with two six-cylinder 300 hp Cummins NT388 engines. Used at British Steel's Ebbw Vale steel works, where it was numbered and named No. 170 *Ebbw*. Preserved at Blaenavon Furnace Sidings, Pontypool & Blaenavon Railway, September 2011.

Corus Steel 1,124 hp Bo-Bo No. 72, built by Hunslet (No. 7283 of 1972) for British Steel's Scunthorpe plant, one of eleven built 1972–73. It has two 562 hp Rolls Royce diesel engines and electric transmission. At Barrow Hill, April 2009.

McEwan Pratt Shunters

McEwan Pratt 0-4-0 petrol shunter No. 680 of 1916, built for Richard, Johnson & Nephew Ltd's Bradford Works, Manchester, and later sold to W. R. Jacob's Aintree Works, Liverpool; preserved at the Dinting Railway Centre, April 1976.

Motor Rail (Simplex) Shunters

Motor Rail & Tramcar Co. Ltd (or Simplex for short) 4wd diesel mechanical shunter No. 2262 of 1924 (rebuilt 1934), *Helen*, at the Foxfield Light Railway, October 1999. *Helen* was built with a White & Poppe petrol engine, but this was replaced in the rebuilding by a Dorman diesel. She was built for the Cornforth Limestone Co. quarry in County Durham, but in 1949 was bought by the Dunlop Rim & Wheel Co. of Coventry. In 1968 it was preserved by the Foxfield Railway.

Ruston & Hornsby Shunters

Ruston & Hornsby 50 hp 0-4-0 diesel mechanical shunters of 1950, built for the 3-foot gauge Parkgate Iron & Steel Co.'s Rotherham Steelworks system as *Midlander*, but re-gauged to 2-foot 3-inches when bought by the Talyllyn Railway; at Towyn Wharf Station, June 1969.

Ruston & Hornsby Type 88DS 0-4-0 diesel mechanical shunter No. 299107 of 1950 with a 88 hp Ruston 3VPH engine. 254 of this type were built. At Lime Firms Ltd's Pentregwenlais Works, Llandybie, Carmarthen, November 1969.

Preserved Ruston & Hornsby Type 165DE 0-4-0 diesel electric shunter No. 424841 of 1960 (ex-*Roman*) with a 150 hp Ruston 6VPHL engine of 165 hp. BR bought two of the mechanical transmission version of this type of loco. At the Foxfield Steam Railway, October 1999.

Ruston & Hornsby Type 48DS 4w diesel mechanical shunter with a 48 hp Ruston & Hornsby engine No. 200793 of 1940, *Gower Princess*. Preserved at Blaenavon Furnace Sidings, Pontypool & Blaenavon Railway, September 2011.

Opposite top: Preserved Ruston & Hornsby Type 88DS 4w diesel mechanical shunter No. 299099 of 1957 with a 88 hp Ruston 3VPH engine. 254 of this type were built. At Tyseley Depot, June 2010.

Opposite bottom: Ruston & Hornsby Type 88DS 4w diesel mechanical shunter No. 338416 of 1953, *Crabtree*, with an 88 hp Ruston 3VPH engine. 254 of this type were built. *Crabtree* was built for the National Oil & Coke Co's works at Erith, Kent, and later sold to British Gypsum, which also used it at Erith. Now preserved at the Electric Railway Museum, Coventry, September 2011.

Ruston & Hornsby Type 165DE 0-4-0 diesel electric shunter No. 268881 of 1950, *Mazda*, with a 150 hp Ruston 6VPHL engine of 165 hp, preserved at the Electric Railway Museum, Coventry, September 2011. BR bought two of the mechanical transmission version of this type of loco. *Mazda* was the first of 164 Type 165DEs to be built. It was used at BTH's Rugby Works, which made Mazda light bulbs.

Preserved Ruston & Hornsby 0-6-0 diesel hydraulic shunter No. 466618 of 1961, No. 429, at Bitton station, Avon Valley Railway, December 2012. The engine is a 275 hp Paxman 6RPHL. This loco is identical to the BR Class 07.

Preserved Rolls-Royce/Sentinel 34t 0-4-0 diesel hydraulic No. 10175 of 1964, with 255 hp Rolls-Royce C6SFL engine, Manchester Ship Canal No. DH16, at Williton, West Somerset Railway, March 2010.

Rolls-Royce/Sentinel 34t 0-4-0 diesel hydraulic No. 10204 of 1965, *Jean*, with 255 hp Rolls-Royce C6SFL engine, at Long Marston, September 2010. The last of a class of '30 tonners' built for the Oxfordshire Ironstone Co. and used at their Wroxton Quarry until its closure in 1968. It was then sold to Stewarts & Lloyds, who used it at their Glendon East, Storefield and Corby quarries, Northants, as No. 8311/03. In 1975 it was sold to the Midland Yorkshire Distilleries at Kilnhurst. No. 10204 had higher gearing than, and minor differences from, the earlier members of the '30 tonners' and effectively acted as a prototype of the next type of 0-4-0 Sentinels.

Sentinel 34t 0-4-0 diesel hydraulic No. 10119 of 1962 with 233 hp Rolls-Royce C6SFL engine, Wabtec No. HO14 *Suzie*, at Long Marston, September 2010.

Rolls-Royce/Sentinel 34t 0-4-0 diesel hydraulic No. 10251 of 1966 with 233 hp Rolls Royce C6SFL engine, Wabtec No. HO21, at Long Marston, September 2010.

Rolls-Royce/Sentinel 48t 0-6-0 diesel hydraulic No. 10213 of 1964 (rebuilt by Thomas Hill 1988) with Rolls Royce 325 hp C8SFL engine. As RMC Roadstone No. 11, *Valiant*, it worked at their Peak Forest site. Now owned by Harry Needle Railroad Company, at Barrow Hill, April 2009.

Opposite top: Sentinel 34t 0-4-0 diesel hydraulic No. 10137 of 1962 with 233 hp Rolls-Royce C6SFL engine, Wabtec No. HO13, at Long Marston, September 2010.

Opposite bottom: Sentinel 74t 650 hp 0-8-0 diesel hydraulic No. 10143 of 1963 with two 325 hp Rolls-Royce C8SFL engines (though removed), Army No. 610 *General Lord Robertson*, at Long Marston, September 2010.

Thomas Hill (Vanguard) Shunters

Thomas Hill diesel hydraulic 0-6-0 No. TH167V of 1966, Creative Solutions No. 01552, with a 325 hp Rolls-Royce C8CFL engine, at Long Marston, September 2010.

Opposite top: Beautifully presented Thomas Hill (Vanguard) 34t 0-4-0 diesel hydraulic with 255 hp Rolls-Royce C6SFL engine No. 319V of 1988, rebuilt by the LH Group at Barton-under-Needwood in 2002. Originally a Sentinel design. MoD No. 01512 (ex-301) *Conductor* was used at the Defence Storage & Distribution Centre at Bicester. Pictured in the rain at Long Marston Open Day, June 2009.

Opposite bottom: Thomas Hill (Vanguard) 0-6-0 diesel hydraulic No. 237V of 1971, Coalite No. 9, powered by a 325 hp Rolls-Royce C8SFL engine, now owned by Harry Needle Railway Company, at Barrow Hill, April 2009.

Believed to be a Thomas Hill 0-6-0 diesel hydraulic, No. 237V of 1971 of HNRC in RFS livery (their No. 9) at Barrow Hill, August 2008.

Vulcan Foundry Shunters

Vulcan Foundry 0-4-0 diesel mechanical shunter No. 5258 of 1945, built for the War Department as Army No. 249/YD10433. At Long Marston, September 2010.

Yorkshire Engine 325 hp 0-6-0 diesel mechanical shunter No. 2760 of 1957, Port of London Authority No. 235 *Bamborough*. In 1971 it was sold to GKN and used at Cardiff Steelworks as No. 372 at Toddington, Gloucestershire–Warwickshire Railway, May 2013. No. 2760 was one of eleven built for the PLA. It has a Rolls-Royce C8SFL engine.

RENFE 5-foot 6-inch gauge 600 hp 0-8-0 diesel hydraulic shunter No. 45 (UIC No. 306-001-9), built by the Yorkshire Engine Co., Sheffield, No. 2892 of 1963. It has two 300 hp Rolls-Royce C8SFL engines. At Madrid Railway Museum, Delicias Station, April 2010. The prototype, *Taurus*, was built in 1961 for heavy shunting, trip freight and local freight (much like the BR Class 14 0-6-0s) and loaned to BR for two years and then withdrawn – what little use for a powerful locomotive. However, some sources suggest that many of the components of the prototype were fitted to the new wider chassis of the Spanish locomotive. The *Taurus* had a very problematical gearbox so RENFE no ordered more. Yorkshire Engine then built two further 'Indus' locos identical to *Taurus* but with a simpler, much more reliable gearbox, for the steel industry. The Indus was a successful design, but unfortunately by 1968 many redundant, nearly new Class 14s were coming onto the market in the UK at little more than scrap value, with the result that the demand for the Indus design among private industry evaporated.

Bibliography

Billinghurst, Colin, *Industrial Locomotives* (Melton Mowbray, Industrial Railway Society, 2009)

King, Ray, *British Industrial Diesel Shunters (Standard Gauge)* (Diss, Barkers Publishing on behalf of the *Traction & Rolling Stock Advertiser*, 2006)

Marsden, Colin J., *The Diesel Shunter* (Oxford, Oxford Publishing Co., 1981)

Marsden, Colin J., 'The Class 14, Class 15, Class 16 & Class 17s' in *Modern Locomotives Illustrated* No. 186 (Dawlish, The Railway Centre.Com Ltd, 2012)

Marsden, Colin J., 'The Small Shunters excluding BR Designs' in *Modern Locomotives Illustrated* No. 195 (Dawlish, The Railway Centre.Com Ltd, 2012)

Marsden, Colin J., 'BR Standard Shunters Classes 08, 09, 10 & 13' in *Modern Locomotives Illustrated* No. 202 (Stamford, Key Publishing Ltd, 2013)